A JAZZ PICTORIAL

A collection of photographs capturing some of the greats of the Jazz & Blues world by

BRIAN FOSKETT

FOREWORD BY DAVE GELLY

Best Wishes

Brian Foskett

I would like to thank Ken Vail for his encouragement and time in putting this book together. Without him, this book would not have happened – well, not yet anyway. Thanks, Ken.

Thanks also to Dave Gelly and Harry Edison for their much appreciated words, and to Rik Goodfellow, Stan Cooper, Bruce Nye and Simon Rawles for the great help they have given over the years.

COVER PHOTOGRAPH
Mr Jazz, Harry 'Sweets' Edison, this time as a member of the Philip Morris Superband appearing at Maastricht Jazz Mecca '91.

Published by Foskett Publishing
Cambridge, England

Copyright © Brian Foskett 1997

ISBN: 0 95311 290 X

Designed by Ken Vail
Printed and bound in the UK by The Burlington Press, Cambridge

When Brian Foskett started taking pictures, more than 30 years ago, the jazz world was a very different place. Virtually all the great names – Hawkins, Getz, Gillespie, Cole – were still alive and would occasionally descend among us. More often than not they would appear in places small enough to be classed as intimate, where they could be heard without the dubious assistance of elaborate PA systems. Young jazz fans today would find it incredible that Sonny Rollins played in a Hampstead pub, or that Roland Kirk plied his bizarre and unique trade in the function room of a suburban roadhouse, or that Peggy Lee appeared nightly at a small and more than slightly tatty West End club. But they did, and because Brian followed them with his camera we can see them doing it.

So much for the purely documentary value of this book. Equally important is the way in which Brian's pictures capture the essence of an artist's style. They look the way they sound. Can't you just hear Cleo Laine's voice when you see his shot of her in full flight? Dexter Gordon, sweating mightily in his mohair suit, Mr B shirt and cufflinks, is a study in concentrated force, just like his playing. And, yes, Stan Getz did sit out on the steps of 39 Gerrard Street between sets, holding court. When he was in the mood he could be charm itself, as Brian's picture brilliantly suggests.

Some of us, a very small circle of friends, have known about Brian Foskett's pictures for years. I have owned prints of Peggy Lee in the rain, Dexter at the Marquee and a few others since shortly after they were taken. But very few have ever been published. Now the secret is out. For every shot in *A Jazz Pictorial* there are dozens, probably hundreds, more. I think we can safely say that, with this book, a major jazz photographer makes his long-overdue debut.

DAVE GELLY

This Book is a Classic. It is a must.

Harry "Sweets" Edison

LOUIS ARMSTRONG

Louis Armstrong in London, having his hair cut in between shows at Hammersmith and relaxing at Finsbury Park Astoria during a Harold Davison UK concert tour in 1962. The thing that tickled me when taking Louis' photo was that, instead of cheese, he said…
S-P-A-G-H-E-T-T-E-E-E !

PEGGY LEE

Peggy Lee on a very wet night in London, leaving the Pigalle night club by taxi after her appearance there in 1961. To my surprise the rain helped to make the shot.

The seductive Miss Lee on stage at London's Royal Albert Hall in 1970.

COUNT BASIE

One of the greatest live jazz experiences of the 60's was Count Basie and his Orchestra, always in good party spirit, featuring the dynamic drumming of Sonny Payne (right) and the tenor solos of Frank Foster (below), who later took over the band.

FLIP PHILLIPS
At 'The March Of Jazz 1997', just off the sands at Clearwater Beach, Florida, some of the jazz greats entertained. Among them, Flip Phillips, 82, and Jerry Jerome, 85, together blew a storm that was reminiscent of the great tenor battles Flip had with Illinois Jacquet, in those JATP days ....
KNOCK OUT!

ILLINOIS JACQUET
The Texas raver playing the Capital Radio Jazz Festival, London, in 1979. He is seen here with that pounding bass player from the old Jay McShann Band, Gene Ramey.

FRANK WESS
*Left: Reacting to the cry of 'Roland Kirk!!'
during a Count Basie UK tour in the early
sixties.*

*Below: Gigging on flute at the Union Chapel,
London, in 1995.*

ROLAND KIRK
*Above: Blind multi-instrumentalist Kirk who
blew everything in sight... out of sight!
Here in a session at the Black Prince, Bexley,
London, 1967.*

JOHN HANDY

Ex-Mingus sideman, John Handy, at a benefit tribute honouring master guitarist Eddie Duran, at Kimball's East in Emeryville, San Francisco, in 1997.

DANNIE RICHMOND

Long-standing Mingus drummer and right-hand man, Dannie Richmond, leading the Mingus Dynasty at the Capital Radio Jazz Festival, Alexandra Palace, London, in 1979.

REGGIE WORKMAN
*Bassist Reggie Workman, onetime member
of the John Coltrane rhythm section, at a
workshop/concert in London, 1997.*

ELVIN JONES
*The amazing Elvin Jones at 70, longtime
associate of John Coltrane, with his Jazz
Machine at the Jazz Bakery in Los
Angeles, 1997.*

DUKE ELLINGTON

Right: In rehearsal for a Sacred Concert at Great St. Mary's Church, Cambridge, England, in 1967.

Above: Leading the orchestra, featuring Lawrence Brown, during a UK tour in the early sixties. The trombone section, seen warming up for the show, are Chuck Connors, Buster Cooper and Lawrence Brown.

SONNY STITT
In one of his last sessions in the UK, Sonny Stitt is seen at the Capital Radio Jazz Festival at Alexandra Palace (Ally Pally) in 1979 where he appeared with Dizzy and Milt Jackson.

DIZZY GILLESPIE

The irrepressible Dizzy Gillespie helping out the rhythm section on congas with his own group at the same Capital Radio Jazz Festival.

GABOR SZABO

The Hungarian guitarist, again at the Capital Radio Jazz Festival in 1979, with the great West Coast drummer Shelly Manne, in a group which also included Jimmy Rowles and Major Holley.

BUDDY RICH
"Drum clinics? What are these places," asked Buddy Rich (left) in 1967, "a place for sick drummers?"

LOUIS BELLSON
With Duke Ellington in 1952 Louis Bellson recorded the famous 'Skin Deep' that led to big bands treating the audience to marathon drum solos. Here showing his skills at another London drum clinic in 1967.

ZOOT SIMS
At the Marquee Jazz Club, a large venue in London's Oxford Street, 1961.

STAN GETZ
Right: Appearing at Ronnie Scott's Gerrard Street club in the early sixties. This club, now affectionately known as 'the old place,' is where it all began for Ronnie.

Above: Relaxing between sets one Sunday afternoon, Getz chats with some good looking girls, real stunners if I remember rightly.

JOHN LEE HOOKER
At the greatest of all London's jazz clubs during the 50's and early 60's, the Flamingo in Wardour Street, Soho, 1961.

SONNY BOY WILLIAMSON
The bluesman who influenced so many of the rock/beat groups in the 60's, not just with his sound but with his sinister charisma. Seen here with the Chris Barber Blues Band at the Marquee, London, 1967.

ALEXIS KORNER
A British bluesman who also had an influence on the groups at this time is seen (above) with a young Art Themen at the Manchester Jazz Festival in 1963.

MICK JAGGER
The Rolling Stones were one of the young groups of the 60's who were influenced by the old blues men. Mick Jagger and the group (left), at the beginning of their great popularity, perform at the Richmond Jazz & Blues Festival in London, 1964.

JIMMY WITHERSPOON
Often, in the 60's, Spoon would appear at the Bull's Head, Barnes, with Dick Morrissey, Phil Seamen and Phil Bates. These sessions will always be remembered as a real rave.

BUCK CLAYTON

Along with Dizzy Gillespie and Bud Freeman, Buck Clayton played the first Daily Mail International Jazz Festival at Belle Vue, Manchester (left), in 1963. Buck appeared with the Humphrey Lyttelton band which featured tenorist Danny Moss.

Above: Buck's mouthpiece causes some interest for Alex Welsh.

WILD BILL DAVISON

In the 60's many New Orleans and Dixieland players came to the UK after the Musician's Union had sorted out an exchange process. They were usually backed by British bands such as Chris Barber, Kenny Ball, Alan Elsdon and the very popular Alex Welsh Band. The Welsh Band are the backing for ex-Condonite Wild Bill Davison (above).

HENRY 'RED' ALLEN
The Alex Welsh Band are again the backing group for Henry 'Red' Allen (right). Note the young Roy Williams.

DEXTER GORDON
Many of the big names booked for Ronnie Scott's Club would play the Marquee on their Sundays off. This is Dexter (left) at the Marquee in 1962.

SONNY ROLLINS
Playing at Klook's Kleek, a popular club at the time, in West Hampstead, North London, in 1967.

BEN WEBSTER

*Big Ben, 'The Brute' as he was known,
played the most passionate tenor that could
make you cry.*

*Right: At the Birmingham Jazz Festival in
the mid-60's, after 'talking motor-bikes' with
a gang of Hells Angels.*

*Below: In a great mood leaving the
Royal Festival Hall, London, after visiting
Ray Charles.*

SCOTT HAMILTON

*Blowing up a storm for Jazz Caravan at the Exchange in
Cambridge, 1991. What a belting session, with a superb
rhythm team comprising Colin Purbrook, piano; Dave Green,
bass; and Allan Ganley, drums.*

ELLA FITZGERALD

Left: Ella at her best with JATP, receiving a hug from Roy Eldridge in between shows at the Odeon, Hammersmith, London, in 1962.

Opposite: Ella making what was to be her final concert appearance in England at the Royal Albert Hall in 1990, with the Count Basie Band under the leadership of Frank Foster.

COLEMAN HAWKINS

Coleman Hawkins taking it easy during a JATP tour of England, with all his requirements at hand.

RAY BROWN

The easily identifiable sound of Ray Brown has been at the forefront of jazz for more than 40 years. Here with his trio, including the very fine young pianist Benny Green and drummer Jeff Hamilton, at the North Sea Jazz Festival in 1993.

KENNY BURRELL

From the 50's, Kenny has always been in the top league of guitarists and has played with everybody who's anybody, including a popular recording stint with Jimmy Smith in the 60's. Here he is with a trio at the 1989 North Sea Jazz Festival.

JOE WILDER

At 75, Joe still has that big tone as he proved at Arbor Records' 'March of Jazz', Clearwater Beach, Florida, 1997. Whether on trumpet or flugelhorn, with plunger mute or plastic cup, he is the complete master.

BUCKY PIZZARELLI
BOB HAGGART

What a rhythm team they make, generating a tight, pounding swing. Together with drummer Joe Ascione they backed much of the great talent at the 'March of Jazz', Clearwater Beach, Florida, 1997.

MILT JACKSON
Taking time out from the Modern Jazz Quartet to lead his own quartet at the North Sea Jazz Festival, Holland, in 1994.

BOBBY HUTCHERSON
Below: An aggressive looking Bobby Hutcherson at the Eddie Duran benefit at Kimball's East, Emeryville, San Francisco, in 1997.

HORACE SILVER
Opposite: The hard bop pianist, composer of 'Sister Sadie,' 'Doodlin',' 'The Preacher' to name a few, came to the Forum, London, in 1996 with his septet.

RAY CHARLES

In full flight (below) at a Capital Radio Jazz Festival in Knebworth Park in 1982.

NAT KING COLE

Caught resting up at the Finsbury Park Astoria during his last tour of the UK with Ted Heath's Band in 1963. Smoking, and coughing badly between shows, he died of cancer in early 1965.

HARRY 'SWEETS' EDISON
At 76, looking like a man half his age, the cool and debonair 'Sweets' is seen with Benny Carter's Swing America at the North Sea Jazz Festival in Holland, 1991.

AL GREY
At the same time, Al Grey shouts his approval for 'Swing America' with rhythm team Marian McPartland (piano), Milt Hinton (bass) and Louis Bellson (drums).

LIONEL HAMPTON
Right: At the outdoor Capital Radio Jazz Festival, Knebworth, England in 1982, Hamp captivated a young audience with his big band's performance of 'Flying Home.'

Below: After being held up in New York, an hour late and jet-lagged, Hamp went straight on stage at the Lewisham Theatre, London, in 1989. He did his whole show and would not leave, telling jokes until the lights went out.

BENNY CARTER

Taking time out to listen to Sweets Edison, Clark Terry, Bob Brookmeyer, Hank Jones and many others at a great 3-day Jazz Inn Hotel Party in Nordwijk, Holland, 1989. Carter was invited as a mystery guest, and nobody knew that he was there, including the musicians.

Above: At the age of 88, with the Tommy Flanagan Trio at the 20th North Sea Jazz Festival in 1995.

GERRY MULLIGAN

Drummer Dave Bailey (above), who came to prominence with Gerry Mulligan, seen here applying that gentle swing during a UK tour in the early 60's.

Right: the rest of the quartet at the same London concert. Left to right: Gerry Mulligan, Bob Brookmeyer and Bill Crow.

Some years later, Gerry (left) with his big band at the Capital Radio Jazz Festival in 1982.

BOB BROOKMEYER
*Along with Clark Terry (Mumbles &
Grumbles), he had one of the most musical
and entertaining groups ever. Just give a listen
to 'The Power of Positive Swinging.' At the
Jazz Inn Party, Holland, in 1989, they got
together for one more blow.*

CLARK TERRY
*Clark is seen, not at the Jazz Inn Party, but
still in Holland at the North Sea Jazz
Festival, 1992, where he was backed by a
trio led by Frans Elsen.*

CHICO HAMILTON
*Chico was responsible for the
unique West Coast jazz quintet
sound of cello and flute in the
50's. Now more into jazz
fusion, he is caught here at the
Jazz Café, London, in 1994.*

JIMMY RUSHING

During a major UK tour in the 60's with Sarah Vaughan and the Count Basie Band. At one time, there were so many musicians backstage at the Finsbury Park Astoria, that a jam session started in the wings, led by Eric Dixon on tenor sax with Mr. Five by Five on camera (right).

JOE WILLIAMS

After leaving the Count Basie Band, Joe went solo and toured the UK in a package with George Shearing's Quintet (below).

Some years on, but still looking good at 70, Joe is seen performing (left) on one of the 12 stages at the mammoth North Sea Jazz Festival at the Hague, Holland, 1989.

OSCAR PETERSON

With his new trio of Sam Jones (bass) and Bobby Durham (drums), Oscar Peterson brings the 1968 UK tour to a close at the Wembley Town Hall.

ED THIGPEN

For many years, Ed Thigpen was associated, along with Ray Brown, with Oscar Peterson's most famous trio. Here he is backing some of the great names at the Jazz Inn Party, Holland, 1989, looking very much the same as he did in the early 60's.

RONNIE SCOTT

After co-leading the Jazz Couriers with Tubby Hayes, Ronnie (and Pete King) opened a jazz club in Gerrard Street, in the heart of Soho, London, in 1959. This is where I took my first shots, on a 35mm Halina camera which cost me £7 19s 6d. For the first time, visiting Americans could be heard in a club atmosphere in this country, and the venue became so popular that in 1965 Ronnie Scott's Jazz Club moved to larger, plusher premises around the corner in Frith Street.

THE OLD PLACE

Many of Britain's finest modern jazz musicians played at Ronnie's cellar club including Tubby Hayes (top), Vic Feldman (above) paying a visit after emigrating to America, Phil Seamen and Jeff Clyne (left) and Stan Tracey with the boss (opposite).

BETTY CARTER
Entertaining the crowd (left) at Maastricht's 1992 Jazz Mecca in Holland.

CARMEN McRAE
The great Carmen (right) depping for Ella Fitzgerald, who was taken ill on arrival in Holland for the 1990 North Sea Jazz Festival.

BING CROSBY
Trying to make a discreet exit down a dark alley after appearing with Bob Hope on ITV's 'Sunday Night at the London Palladium' in 1961. As you can see, I wasn't the only one to find him.

FRANK SINATRA
Mack the Knife has Sinatra sneaking round the corner at London's Royal Albert Hall during 'The Ultimate Event,' a grand world tour with Sammy Davis Jr and Liza Minnelli in 1989.

JIMMY COBB
Drummer with the great Miles Davis rhythm section that included Wynton Kelly and Paul Chambers, Jimmy Cobb is seen opposite with Nat Adderley's group at the Jazz Café, London, 1991.

JOHNNY GRIFFIN
Together with Wes Montgomery and the above rhythm section, Johnny Griffin made a classic live recording in the 60's called 'Full House.' In the photograph (right) the exuberant 'Little Giant' is playing with young Jason Rebello at Dingwall's, Camden Town, London, in 1994.

BUD SHANK

One of the most popular West Coast musicians of the 50's cool school, recording with his own groups, Shorty Rogers, and the Marty Paich Dektette. In the 70's came the LA4, with Laurindo Almeida (guitar), Ray Brown (bass), Shelly Manne or Jeff Hamilton (drums) plus the alto and some great flute from Bud Shank. Terrific stuff! He is seen here in Peterborough, during a UK tour in 1995.

JACKIE McLEAN

Originally influenced by Charlie Parker and later by Ornette Coleman, Jackie brought his unique style of playing to the Jazz Café, Camden Town, London, in 1991.

ROY HARGROVE

A young player making his mark on the scene, seen here blowing an encore at the North Sea Jazz Festival in 1994. Roy and his quintet were joined by the tenors of Johnny Griffin and Joshua Redman.

NAT ADDERLEY

With his brother Cannonball, he co-led an exciting, funky group in the late 50's and early 60's which also featured the talents of Bobby Timmons, Sam Jones and Louis Hayes. He is seen here at the 1994 North Sea Jazz Festival with the Riverside Reunion Band which included Jimmy Heath, Tommy Flanagan and Bob Cranshaw.

MILES DAVIS

Just before its demise, the famous Miles Davis Quintet with Wayne Shorter, Herbie Hancock, Ron Carter and Tony Williams played London (left) as part of the Newport Jazz Festival (Expo 67). Miles later ventured into jazz-rock fusions.

KENNY GARRETT

Kenny played a major role in Miles' late 80's bands and is seen here (below) with his sextet at the 1992 Maastricht Jazz Mecca, a year after Miles' death.

J. J. JOHNSON
In 1993, trombone legend J. J. Johnson made a rare visit to Europe and played the North Sea Jazz Festival, fronting a quintet with Ralph Moore.

MAX ROACH
The great bebop drummer from the Charlie Parker era gave a workshop/concert (below) with Archie Shepp at the Queen Elizabeth Hall, London, in 1996.

WAYNE SHORTER
Wayne eventually took over from John Coltrane with the Miles Davis group, succeeding a long line of hopefuls that included Hank Mobley, Sonny Stitt and George Coleman. Here he is on soprano sax with his fusion group at Maastricht's 1995 Music Nights.

TONY WILLIAMS

Tony had everyone talking when, only 17, he took over the Miles Davis drum chair from Jimmy Cobb. His new approach and fantastic technique was the sparkplug for another great rhythm section with Herbie Hancock and Ron Carter. Here he is leading his own group at the Jazz Café, London, in 1991. He died suddenly, aged only 52, in 1997 .

HERBIE HANCOCK

Herbie is seen here leading his trio, Dave Holland (bass) and Gene Jackson (drums), at the Grand, Clapham, London, in 1995.

NINA SIMONE
With her special mystique, Nina puts a spell on the audience at the 1992 Jazz Mecca in Maastricht, Holland.

CLEO LAINE
The ageless Cleo (right) singing at the 1995 Brecon Jazz Festival with the Dankworth Generation Band in support.

FREDDIE HUBBARD
A flamboyant Freddie (left) at Cambridge University's famous Union Debating Chamber during a tour with Ronnie Scott in 1967.

LEE MORGAN
A great player who would have become even greater if a lady friend hadn't shot him dead when he was only 33. He is seen backstage (right) as one of Art Blakey's Jazz Messengers in 1961.

BROTHER JACK McDUFF

The 1991 Jazz Mecca at Maastricht reunited Jack McDuff with his original group – Red Holloway (tenor), Joe Dukes (drums), and guitarist Phil Upchurch taking the place of George Benson.

JIMMY SMITH

The most famous of all jazz organists, particularly in the 60's, with hits including 'Walk On The Wild Side.' In 1994 he came to Dingwall's in London with a group comprising Herman Riley (tenor sax) and drummer Jimmie Smith (no relation).

STANLEY TURRENTINE

His hard blowing sound was often featured with organ based groups like Jimmy Smith and Shirley Scott whom he married. He came to the North Sea Jazz Festival with a quintet, minus organ, in 1993.

TERENCE BLANCHARD
The young trumpeter made quite an impression with his quintet at the 1994 North Sea Jazz Festival.

WYNTON MARSALIS
The classically trained, all-round trumpeter from New Orleans. His style, covering all aspects and rhythms of jazz, was well featured in 1993 at The Grand, Clapham, London, with a septet featuring reedmen Wes Anderson and Walter Blanding, trombonist Wycliffe Gordon, pianist Eric Reed, bassist Reginald Veal and drummer Herlin Riley.

ART BLAKEY
In 1968, at London's Hammersmith Odeon, Elvin Jones, Max Roach, Sonny Murray and Art Blakey (left) presented a drum workshop, appearing with their own groups and finishing with a drum battle.

JOSHUA REDMAN
Blowing up a storm (left) and musing over events (right), at the 1995 North Sea Jazz Festival.

DAVID SANCHEZ
As a member of Slide Hampton's Jazz Masters with Antonio Hart, Robin Eubanks and veteran James Moody, David Sanchez impressed everybody at the 1993 North Sea Jazz Festival.

GEORGE MELLY
Our 'Mr Bessie Smith' has been singing
the blues in a rather camp fashion for the
past 40 years. Seen here giving a TV
interview during London's Soho Jazz
Festival in 1993.